Hangry

Dictionary Definition
Blank Recipe Book
(8.5 x 11 Inches)

These Recipes Belong To:

_____

BONUS: Link to digital download on last page

Table of Contents

Table of Contents

Name: _____

Prep-Time	Cook-Time	Serves

Source:

☐ Breakfast ☐ Lunch ☐ Dinner ☐ Dessert ☐ O

Ingredients

☐ ....
☐ ....
☐ ....
☐ ....
☐ ....
☐ ....
☐ ....
☐ ....
☐ ....
☐ ....
☐ ....
☐ ....
☐ ....
☐ ....
☐ ....

Directions

1. ....

2. ....

3. ....

4. ....

5. ....

6. ....

7. ....

8. ....

9. ....

Notes

10. ....

Difficulty: *Easy   Medium   Hard*

Rating: ☆ ☆ ☆ ☆ ☆

ame: _____

urce:

Prep-Time   Cook-Time   Serves

Breakfast   □ Lunch   □ Dinner   □ Dessert   □ Other

Directions

Ingredients

□ ....
□ ....
□ ....
□ ....
□ ....
□ ....
□ ....
□ ....
□ ....
□ ....
□ ....
□ ....
□ ....
□ ....
□ ....

Notes

Difficulty: *Easy*   *Medium*   *Hard*

Rating: ☆ ☆ ☆ ☆ ☆

Name: _____

Prep-Time   Cook-Time   Serves

Source:

☐ Breakfast   ☐ Lunch   ☐ Dinner   ☐ Dessert   ☐ O

Ingredients

☐ ....
☐ ....
☐ ....
☐ ....
☐ ....
☐ ....
☐ ....
☐ ....
☐ ....
☐ ....
☐ ....
☐ ....
☐ ....
☐ ....
☐ ....

Directions

1. ....

2. ....

3. ....

4. ....

5. ....

6. ....

7. ....

8. ....

9. ....

Notes

....
....
....
....
....
....
....
....
....
....

Difficulty: *Easy   Medium   Hard*

Rating: ☆ ☆ ☆ ☆ ☆

10. ....

ame: _____

urce:

Prep-Time   Cook-Time   Serves

Breakfast   ☐ Lunch   ☐ Dinner   ☐ Dessert   ☐ Other

Directions

Ingredients

☐ ....
☐ ....
☐ ....
☐ ....
☐ ....
☐ ....
☐ ....
☐ ....
☐ ....
☐ ....
☐ ....
☐ ....
☐ ....
☐ ....

Notes

Difficulty: *Easy*   *Medium*   *Hard*

Rating: ☆ ☆ ☆ ☆ ☆

Name: _____

Prep-Time	Cook-Time	Serves

Source:

☐ Breakfast ☐ Lunch ☐ Dinner ☐ Dessert ☐ O

Ingredients

☐ ....
☐ ....
☐ ....
☐ ....
☐ ....
☐ ....
☐ ....
☐ ....
☐ ....
☐ ....
☐ ....
☐ ....
☐ ....
☐ ....
☐ ....

Notes

....
....
....
....
....
....
....
....
....
....

Difficulty: *Easy   Medium   Hard*

Rating: ☆ ☆ ☆ ☆ ☆

Directions

1. ....

2. ....

3. ....

4. ....

5. ....

6. ....

7. ....

8. ....

9. ....

10. ....

ame: _____

urce: _____

☐ Breakfast ☐ Lunch ☐ Dinner ☐ Dessert ☐ Other

Prep-Time   Cook-Time   Serves

Directions

Ingredients

☐ ....
☐ ....
☐ ....
☐ ....
☐ ....
☐ ....
☐ ....
☐ ....
☐ ....
☐ ....
☐ ....
☐ ....
☐ ....
☐ ....

Notes

Difficulty: *Easy*   *Medium*   *Hard*

Rating: ☆ ☆ ☆ ☆ ☆

Name: _____

Prep-Time   Cook-Time   Serves

☐ Breakfast   ☐ Lunch   ☐ Dinner   ☐ Dessert   ☐ O

Ingredients

☐
☐
☐
☐
☐
☐
☐
☐
☐
☐
☐
☐
☐
☐

Directions

1.

2.

3.

4.

5.

6.

7.

8.

9.

Notes

Difficulty: *Easy   Medium   Hard*

Rating: ☆ ☆ ☆ ☆ ☆

10.

ame: _____

urce:

Prep-Time   Cook-Time   Serves

☐ Breakfast   ☐ Lunch   ☐ Dinner   ☐ Dessert   ☐ Other

Directions

Ingredients

☐ ....
☐ ....
☐ ....
☐ ....
☐ ....
☐ ....
☐ ....
☐ ....
☐ ....
☐ ....
☐ ....
☐ ....
☐ ....
☐ ....
☐ ....

Notes

Difficulty: *Easy   Medium   Hard*

Rating: ☆ ☆ ☆ ☆ ☆

Name: _____

Prep-Time	Cook-Time	Serves

☐ Breakfast   ☐ Lunch   ☐ Dinner   ☐ Dessert   ☐ O

Ingredients

☐ ....
☐ ....
☐ ....
☐ ....
☐ ....
☐ ....
☐ ....
☐ ....
☐ ....
☐ ....
☐ ....
☐ ....
☐ ....
☐ ....
☐ ....

Directions

1.

2.

3.

4.

5.

6.

7.

8.

9.

Notes

....
....
....
....
....
....
....
....
....
....

Difficulty: *Easy   Medium   Hard*

Rating: ☆ ☆ ☆ ☆ ☆

10.

ame: _____

urce:

□ Breakfast □ Lunch □ Dinner □ Dessert □ Other

Prep-Time   Cook-Time   Serves

Directions

Ingredients

□ ....
□ ....
□ ....
□ ....
□ ....
□ ....
□ ....
□ ....
□ ....
□ ....
□ ....
□ ....
□ ....
□ ....
□ ....

Notes

Difficulty: *Easy   Medium   Hard*

Rating: ☆ ☆ ☆ ☆ ☆

Name: _____

Prep-Time   Cook-Time   Serves

Source:

☐ Breakfast   ☐ Lunch   ☐ Dinner   ☐ Dessert   ☐ O

Ingredients

☐ ....
☐ ....
☐ ....
☐ ....
☐ ....
☐ ....
☐ ....
☐ ....
☐ ....
☐ ....
☐ ....
☐ ....
☐ ....
☐ ....
☐ ....

Notes

Directions

1.

2.

3.

4.

5.

6.

7.

8.

9.

10.

Difficulty: *Easy   Medium   Hard*

Rating: ☆ ☆ ☆ ☆ ☆

ame: _____

urce:

Prep-Time   Cook-Time   Serves

☐ Breakfast   ☐ Lunch   ☐ Dinner   ☐ Dessert   ☐ Other

Directions

Ingredients

☐ ....
☐ ....
☐ ....
☐ ....
☐ ....
☐ ....
☐ ....
☐ ....
☐ ....
☐ ....
☐ ....
☐ ....
☐ ....
☐ ....

Notes

Difficulty: *Easy   Medium   Hard*

Rating: ☆ ☆ ☆ ☆ ☆

Name: _____

Prep-Time   Cook-Time   Serves

☐ Breakfast   ☐ Lunch   ☐ Dinner   ☐ Dessert   ☐ O

Ingredients

☐ ....
☐ ....
☐ ....
☐ ....
☐ ....
☐ ....
☐ ....
☐ ....
☐ ....
☐ ....
☐ ....
☐ ....
☐ ....
☐ ....
☐ ....

Notes

....
....
....
....
....
....
....
....

Difficulty: *Easy   Medium   Hard*

Rating: ☆ ☆ ☆ ☆ ☆

Directions

1.

2.

3.

4.

5.

6.

7.

8.

9.

10.

ame: _____

urce:

Prep-Time   Cook-Time   Serves

Breakfast   ☐ Lunch   ☐ Dinner   ☐ Dessert   ☐ Other

Directions

Ingredients

☐
☐
☐
☐
☐
☐
☐
☐
☐
☐
☐
☐
☐
☐
☐

Notes

Difficulty: *Easy   Medium   Hard*

Rating: ☆ ☆ ☆ ☆ ☆

Name: _____

Prep-Time   Cook-Time   Serves

☐ Breakfast   ☐ Lunch   ☐ Dinner   ☐ Dessert   ☐ O

Ingredients

☐ ....
☐ ....
☐ ....
☐ ....
☐ ....
☐ ....
☐ ....
☐ ....
☐ ....
☐ ....
☐ ....
☐ ....
☐ ....
☐ ....
☐ ....

Notes

....
....
....
....
....
....
....
....
....
....

Difficulty: *Easy   Medium   Hard*

Rating: ☆ ☆ ☆ ☆ ☆

Directions

1. ....

2. ....

3. ....

4. ....

5. ....

6. ....

7. ....

8. ....

9. ....

10. ....

me: _____

rce:

eakfast ☐ Lunch ☐ Dinner ☐ Dessert ☐ Other

Prep-Time   Cook-Time   Serves

Directions

Ingredients

☐
☐
☐
☐
☐
☐
☐
☐
☐
☐
☐
☐
☐
☐
☐

Notes

Difficulty: *Easy   Medium   Hard*

Rating: ☆ ☆ ☆ ☆ ☆

Name: _____

Prep-Time   Cook-Time   Serves

☐ Breakfast   ☐ Lunch   ☐ Dinner   ☐ Dessert   ☐ O

Ingredients

☐ ....
☐ ....
☐ ....
☐ ....
☐ ....
☐ ....
☐ ....
☐ ....
☐ ....
☐ ....
☐ ....
☐ ....
☐ ....
☐ ....
☐ ....

Notes

....
....
....
....
....
....
....
....
....
....
....

Difficulty: *Easy   Medium   Hard*

Rating: · ☆ ☆ ☆ ☆ ☆

Directions

1.
....

2.
....

3.
....

4.
....

5.
....

6.
....

7.
....

8.
....

9.
....

10.
....

ame: _____

urce:

Prep-Time   Cook-Time   Serves

□ Breakfast   □ Lunch   □ Dinner   □ Dessert   □ Other

Directions

Ingredients

□
□
□
□
□
□
□
□
□
□
□
□
□
□
□

Notes

Difficulty: *Easy*   *Medium*   *Hard*

Rating: ☆ ☆ ☆ ☆ ☆

Name: _____

Prep-Time   Cook-Time   Serves

☐ Breakfast   ☐ Lunch   ☐ Dinner   ☐ Dessert   ☐ O

Ingredients

☐ ....
☐ ....
☐ ....
☐ ....
☐ ....
☐ ....
☐ ....
☐ ....
☐ ....
☐ ....
☐ ....
☐ ....
☐ ....
☐ ....
☐ ....

Notes

....
....
....
....
....
....
....
....
....

Difficulty: *Easy   Medium   Hard*

Rating: ☆ ☆ ☆ ☆ ☆

Directions

1.

2.

3.

4.

5.

6.

7.

8.

9.

10.

ame: _____

urce:

□ Breakfast   □ Lunch   □ Dinner   □ Dessert   □ Other

Prep-Time   Cook-Time   Serves

Directions

Ingredients

□
□
□
□
□
□
□
□
□
□
□
□
□
□
□

Notes

Difficulty: *Easy   Medium   Hard*

Rating: ☆ ☆ ☆ ☆ ☆

Name: _____

Prep-Time   Cook-Time   Serves

Source:

☐ Breakfast   ☐ Lunch   ☐ Dinner   ☐ Dessert   ☐

Ingredients

☐ ....
☐ ....
☐ ....
☐ ....
☐ ....
☐ ....
☐ ....
☐ ....
☐ ....
☐ ....
☐ ....
☐ ....
☐ ....
☐ ....
☐ ....

Notes

Directions

1.

2.

3.

4.

5.

6.

7.

8.

9.

10.

Difficulty: *Easy*   *Medium*   *Hard*

Rating: ☆ ☆ ☆ ☆ ☆

ame: _____

urce:

☐ Breakfast   ☐ Lunch   ☐ Dinner   ☐ Dessert   ☐ Other

Prep-Time	Cook-Time	Serves

Directions

Ingredients

☐ ....
☐ ....
☐ ....
☐ ....
☐ ....
☐ ....
☐ ....
☐ ....
☐ ....
☐ ....
☐ ....
☐ ....
☐ ....
☐ ....
☐ ....

Notes

Difficulty: *Easy*   *Medium*   *Hard*

Rating: ☆ ☆ ☆ ☆ ☆

Name: _____

Prep-Time   Cook-Time   Serves

Source:

☐ Breakfast   ☐ Lunch   ☐ Dinner   ☐ Dessert   ☐ O

Ingredients

☐ ....
☐ ....
☐ ....
☐ ....
☐ ....
☐ ....
☐ ....
☐ ....
☐ ....
☐ ....
☐ ....
☐ ....
☐ ....
☐ ....
☐ ....

Notes

....
....
....
....
....
....
....
....
....
....

Difficulty: *Easy   Medium   Hard*

Rating: ☆ ☆ ☆ ☆ ☆

Directions

1. ....

2. ....

3. ....

4. ....

5. ....

6. ....

7. ....

8. ....

9. ....

10. ....

ame: _____

urce:

Prep-Time   Cook-Time   Serves

☐ Breakfast   ☐ Lunch   ☐ Dinner   ☐ Dessert   ☐ Other

Directions

Ingredients

☐
☐
☐
☐
☐
☐
☐
☐
☐
☐
☐
☐
☐
☐
☐

Notes

Difficulty: *Easy*   *Medium*   *Hard*

Rating: ☆ ☆ ☆ ☆ ☆

Name: _____

Prep-Time   Cook-Time   Serves

Source:

☐ Breakfast   ☐ Lunch   ☐ Dinner   ☐ Dessert   ☐ O

Ingredients

☐ ....
☐ ....
☐ ....
☐ ....
☐ ....
☐ ....
☐ ....
☐ ....
☐ ....
☐ ....
☐ ....
☐ ....
☐ ....
☐ ....
☐ ....

Notes

Directions

1.
2.
3.
4.
5.
6.
7.
8.
9.
10.

Difficulty: *Easy   Medium   Hard*

Rating: ☆ ☆ ☆ ☆ ☆

ame: _____

urce:

Prep-Time   Cook-Time   Serves

☐ Breakfast   ☐ Lunch   ☐ Dinner   ☐ Dessert   ☐ Other

Directions

Ingredients

☐
☐
☐
☐
☐
☐
☐
☐
☐
☐
☐
☐
☐
☐

Notes

Difficulty: *Easy   Medium   Hard*

Rating: ☆ ☆ ☆ ☆ ☆

Name: _____

Prep-Time	Cook-Time	Serves

☐ Breakfast ☐ Lunch ☐ Dinner ☐ Dessert ☐ O

Ingredients

☐ ....
☐ ....
☐ ....
☐ ....
☐ ....
☐ ....
☐ ....
☐ ....
☐ ....
☐ ....
☐ ....
☐ ....
☐ ....
☐ ....
☐ ....

Notes

....
....
....
....
....
....
....
....

Difficulty: *Easy   Medium   Hard*

Rating: ☆ ☆ ☆ ☆ ☆

Directions

1. ....

2. ....

3. ....

4. ....

5. ....

6. ....

7. ....

8. ....

9. ....

10. ....

ame: _____

urce:

☐ Lunch   ☐ Dinner   ☐ Dessert   ☐ Other

Prep-Time   Cook-Time   Serves

Directions

Ingredients

☐
☐
☐
☐
☐
☐
☐
☐
☐
☐
☐
☐
☐
☐
☐

Notes

Difficulty: *Easy*   *Medium*   *Hard*

Rating: ☆ ☆ ☆ ☆ ☆

Name: _____

Prep-Time	Cook-Time	Serves

☐ Breakfast ☐ Lunch ☐ Dinner ☐ Dessert ☐ O

Ingredients

☐ ....
☐ ....
☐ ....
☐ ....
☐ ....
☐ ....
☐ ....
☐ ....
☐ ....
☐ ....
☐ ....
☐ ....
☐ ....
☐ ....
☐ ....

Directions

1.
....

2.
....

3.
....

4.
....

5.
....

6.
....

7.
....

8.
....

9.
....

10.
....

Notes

....
....
....
....
....
....
....
....

Difficulty: *Easy*   *Medium*   *Hard*

Rating: ☆ ☆ ☆ ☆ ☆

ame: _____

urce:

Prep-Time   Cook-Time   Serves

☐ Breakfast   ☐ Lunch   ☐ Dinner   ☐ Dessert   ☐ Other

Directions

Ingredients

☐
☐
☐
☐
☐
☐
☐
☐
☐
☐
☐
☐
☐
☐
☐

Notes

Difficulty: *Easy*   *Medium*   *Hard*

Rating: ☆ ☆ ☆ ☆ ☆

Name: _____

Prep-Time   Cook-Time   Serves

☐ Breakfast   ☐ Lunch   ☐ Dinner   ☐ Dessert   ☐ O

Ingredients

☐ ....
☐ ....
☐ ....
☐ ....
☐ ....
☐ ....
☐ ....
☐ ....
☐ ....
☐ ....
☐ ....
☐ ....
☐ ....
☐ ....
☐ ....

Directions

1.
....

2.
....

3.
....

4.
....

5.
....

6.
....

7.
....

8.
....

9.
....

Notes

....
....
....
....
....
....
....
....

Difficulty: *Easy   Medium   Hard*

Rating: ☆ ☆ ☆ ☆ ☆

10.
....

ame: _____

urce: _____

Prep-Time   Cook-Time   Serves

□ Breakfast   □ Lunch   □ Dinner   □ Dessert   □ Other

Directions

Ingredients

□
□
□
□
□
□
□
□
□
□
□
□
□
□
□

Notes

Difficulty: *Easy*   *Medium*   *Hard*

Rating: ☆ ☆ ☆ ☆ ☆

Name: _____

Prep-Time   Cook-Time   Serves

Source:

☐ Breakfast   ☐ Lunch   ☐ Dinner   ☐ Dessert   ☐ O

Ingredients

☐ ....
☐ ....
☐ ....
☐ ....
☐ ....
☐ ....
☐ ....
☐ ....
☐ ....
☐ ....
☐ ....
☐ ....
☐ ....
☐ ....
☐ ....

Directions

1. ....

2. ....

3. ....

4. ....

5. ....

6. ....

7. ....

8. ....

9. ....

Notes

10. ....

Difficulty: *Easy   Medium   Hard*

Rating: ☆ ☆ ☆ ☆ ☆

ame: _____

urce:

Prep-Time   Cook-Time   Serves

☐ Breakfast   ☐ Lunch   ☐ Dinner   ☐ Dessert   ☐ Other

Directions

Ingredients

☐ ....
☐ ....
☐ ....
☐ ....
☐ ....
☐ ....
☐ ....
☐ ....
☐ ....
☐ ....
☐ ....
☐ ....
☐ ....
☐ ....
☐ ....

Notes

Difficulty: *Easy   Medium   Hard*

Rating: ☆ ☆ ☆ ☆ ☆

Name: _____

Prep-Time   Cook-Time   Serves

Source:

☐ Breakfast   ☐ Lunch   ☐ Dinner   ☐ Dessert   ☐ O

Ingredients

☐ ....
☐ ....
☐ ....
☐ ....
☐ ....
☐ ....
☐ ....
☐ ....
☐ ....
☐ ....
☐ ....
☐ ....
☐ ....
☐ ....
☐ ....

Notes

....
....
....
....
....
....
....
....

Difficulty: *Easy   Medium   Hard*

Rating: ☆ ☆ ☆ ☆ ☆

Directions

1. ....

2. ....

3. ....

4. ....

5. ....

6. ....

7. ....

8. ....

9. ....

10. ....

ame: _____

urce:

Prep-Time   Cook-Time   Serves

Breakfast   ☐ Lunch   ☐ Dinner   ☐ Dessert   ☐ Other

Directions

Ingredients

☐
☐
☐
☐
☐
☐
☐
☐
☐
☐
☐
☐
☐
☐
☐

Notes

Difficulty: *Easy*   *Medium*   *Hard*

Rating: ☆ ☆ ☆ ☆ ☆

Name: _____

Prep-Time	Cook-Time	Serves

☐ Breakfast ☐ Lunch ☐ Dinner ☐ Dessert ☐ O

Ingredients

☐ ....
☐ ....
☐ ....
☐ ....
☐ ....
☐ ....
☐ ....
☐ ....
☐ ....
☐ ....
☐ ....
☐ ....
☐ ....
☐ ....
☐ ....

Notes

....
....
....
....
....
....
....
....

Difficulty: *Easy Medium Hard*

Rating: ☆ ☆ ☆ ☆ ☆

Directions

1.

2.

3.

4.

5.

6.

7.

8.

9.

10.

ame: _____

urce:

Prep-Time   Cook-Time   Serves

☐ Breakfast   ☐ Lunch   ☐ Dinner   ☐ Dessert   ☐ Other

Directions

Ingredients

☐
☐
☐
☐
☐
☐
☐
☐
☐
☐
☐
☐
☐
☐
☐

Notes

Difficulty: *Easy   Medium   Hard*

Rating: ☆ ☆ ☆ ☆ ☆

Name: _____

Prep-Time   Cook-Time   Serves

Source:

☐ Breakfast   ☐ Lunch   ☐ Dinner   ☐ Dessert   ☐ O

Ingredients

☐ ....
☐ ....
☐ ....
☐ ....
☐ ....
☐ ....
☐ ....
☐ ....
☐ ....
☐ ....
☐ ....
☐ ....
☐ ....
☐ ....
☐ ....

Notes

Directions

1.

2.

3.

4.

5.

6.

7.

8.

9.

10.

Difficulty: *Easy   Medium   Hard*

Rating: ☆ ☆ ☆ ☆ ☆

ame: _____

urce:

Prep-Time   Cook-Time   Serves

☐reakfast   ☐ Lunch   ☐ Dinner   ☐ Dessert   ☐ Other

Directions

Ingredients

☐
☐
☐
☐
☐
☐
☐
☐
☐
☐
☐
☐
☐
☐
☐

Notes

Difficulty: *Easy   Medium   Hard*

Rating: ☆ ☆ ☆ ☆ ☆

Name: _____

Prep-Time	Cook-Time	Serves

Source:

☐ Breakfast   ☐ Lunch   ☐ Dinner   ☐ Dessert   ☐ O

Ingredients

☐ ....
☐ ....
☐ ....
☐ ....
☐ ....
☐ ....
☐ ....
☐ ....
☐ ....
☐ ....
☐ ....
☐ ....
☐ ....
☐ ....
☐ ....

Notes

Directions

1.

2.

3.

4.

5.

6.

7.

8.

9.

10.

Difficulty: *Easy   Medium   Hard*

Rating: ☆ ☆ ☆ ☆ ☆

ame: _____

urce:

□ Breakfast   □ Lunch   □ Dinner   □ Dessert   □ Other

Prep-Time	Cook-Time	Serves

Directions

Ingredients

□
□
□
□
□
□
□
□
□
□
□
□
□
□
□

Notes

Difficulty: *Easy*   *Medium*   *Hard*

Rating: ☆ ☆ ☆ ☆ ☆

Name: _____

Prep-Time　　Cook-Time　　Serves

Source:

☐ Breakfast　☐ Lunch　☐ Dinner　☐ Dessert　☐ O

Ingredients

☐ ....
☐ ....
☐ ....
☐ ....
☐ ....
☐ ....
☐ ....
☐ ....
☐ ....
☐ ....
☐ ....
☐ ....
☐ ....
☐ ....
☐ ....

Notes

....
....
....
....
....
....
....
....
....
....

Difficulty: *Easy　Medium　Hard*

Rating: ☆ ☆ ☆ ☆ ☆

Directions

1.
2.
3.
4.
5.
6.
7.
8.
9.
10.

ame: _____

urce:

Breakfast ☐ Lunch ☐ Dinner ☐ Dessert ☐ Other

| Prep-Time | Cook-Time | Serves |

Directions

Ingredients

☐
☐
☐
☐
☐
☐
☐
☐
☐
☐
☐
☐
☐
☐
☐

Notes

Difficulty: *Easy   Medium   Hard*

Rating: ☆ ☆ ☆ ☆ ☆

Name: _____

Prep-Time	Cook-Time	Serves

☐ Breakfast   ☐ Lunch   ☐ Dinner   ☐ Dessert   ☐ O

Ingredients

☐ ....
☐ ....
☐ ....
☐ ....
☐ ....
☐ ....
☐ ....
☐ ....
☐ ....
☐ ....
☐ ....
☐ ....
☐ ....
☐ ....
☐ ....

Notes

....
....
....
....
....
....
....
....
....

Difficulty: *Easy*   *Medium*   *Hard*

Rating: ☆ ☆ ☆ ☆ ☆

Directions

1. ....

2. ....

3. ....

4. ....

5. ....

6. ....

7. ....

8. ....

9. ....

10. ....

me: _____

rce:

Prep-Time   Cook-Time   Serves

☐ eakfast   ☐ Lunch   ☐ Dinner   ☐ Dessert   ☐ Other

Directions

Ingredients

☐
☐
☐
☐
☐
☐
☐
☐
☐
☐
☐
☐
☐
☐

Notes

Difficulty: *Easy*   *Medium*   *Hard*

Rating: ☆ ☆ ☆ ☆ ☆

Name: _____

Prep-Time	Cook-Time	Serves

Source:

☐ Breakfast   ☐ Lunch   ☐ Dinner   ☐ Dessert   ☐ O

Ingredients

☐ ....
☐ ....
☐ ....
☐ ....
☐ ....
☐ ....
☐ ....
☐ ....
☐ ....
☐ ....
☐ ....
☐ ....
☐ ....
☐ ....
☐ ....

Notes

....
....
....
....
....
....
....
....
....
....

Difficulty: *Easy   Medium   Hard*

Rating: ☆ ☆ ☆ ☆ ☆

Directions

1.

2.

3.

4.

5.

6.

7.

8.

9.

10.

ame: _____

urce:

□ Breakfast □ Lunch □ Dinner □ Dessert □ Other

Prep-Time   Cook-Time   Serves

Directions

Ingredients

□
□
□
□
□
□
□
□
□
□
□
□
□
□
□

Notes

Difficulty: *Easy   Medium   Hard*

Rating: ☆ ☆ ☆ ☆ ☆

Name: _____

Prep-Time   Cook-Time   Serves

□ Breakfast   □ Lunch   □ Dinner   □ Dessert   □ O

Ingredients

□ ....
□ ....
□ ....
□ ....
□ ....
□ ....
□ ....
□ ....
□ ....
□ ....
□ ....
□ ....
□ ....
□ ....
□ ....

Notes

....
....
....
....
....
....
....
....
....
....
....

Difficulty: *Easy   Medium   Hard*

Rating: ☆ ☆ ☆ ☆ ☆

Directions

1.
....

2.
....

3.
....

4.
....

5.
....

6.
....

7.
....

8.
....

9.
....

10.
....

me: _____

rce:

eakfast   ☐ Lunch   ☐ Dinner   ☐ Dessert   ☐ Other

Prep-Time   Cook-Time   Serves

Directions

Ingredients

☐
☐
☐
☐
☐
☐
☐
☐
☐
☐
☐
☐
☐
☐
☐

Notes

Difficulty: *Easy   Medium   Hard*

Rating: ☆ ☆ ☆ ☆ ☆

Name: _____

Prep-Time	Cook-Time	Serves

☐ Breakfast   ☐ Lunch   ☐ Dinner   ☐ Dessert   ☐ O

Ingredients

☐ ....
☐ ....
☐ ....
☐ ....
☐ ....
☐ ....
☐ ....
☐ ....
☐ ....
☐ ....
☐ ....
☐ ....
☐ ....
☐ ....
☐ ....

Notes

....
....
....
....
....
....
....
....
....
....
....

Difficulty: *Easy*   *Medium*   *Hard*

Rating: ☆ ☆ ☆ ☆ ☆

Directions

1.

2.

3.

4.

5.

6.

7.

8.

9.

10.

ame: _____

urce:

Prep-Time   Cook-Time   Serves

☐ Breakfast ☐ Lunch ☐ Dinner ☐ Dessert ☐ Other

Directions

Ingredients

☐ ....
☐ ....
☐ ....
☐ ....
☐ ....
☐ ....
☐ ....
☐ ....
☐ ....
☐ ....
☐ ....
☐ ....
☐ ....
☐ ....
☐ ....

Notes

Difficulty: *Easy*   *Medium*   *Hard*

Rating: ☆ ☆ ☆ ☆ ☆

Name: _____

Prep-Time	Cook-Time	Serves

☐ Breakfast ☐ Lunch ☐ Dinner ☐ Dessert ☐ O

Ingredients

☐ ....
☐ ....
☐ ....
☐ ....
☐ ....
☐ ....
☐ ....
☐ ....
☐ ....
☐ ....
☐ ....
☐ ....
☐ ....
☐ ....
☐ ....

Notes

....
....
....
....
....
....
....
....
....

Difficulty: *Easy   Medium   Hard*

Rating: ☆ ☆ ☆ ☆ ☆

Directions

1. ....

2. ....

3. ....

4. ....

5. ....

6. ....

7. ....

8. ....

9. ....

10. ....

ame: _____

Recipe #54

urce:

☐ Breakfast ☐ Lunch ☐ Dinner ☐ Dessert ☐ Other

Prep-Time   Cook-Time   Serves

Directions

Ingredients

☐
☐
☐
☐
☐
☐
☐
☐
☐
☐
☐
☐
☐
☐
☐

Notes

Difficulty: *Easy   Medium   Hard*

Rating: ☆ ☆ ☆ ☆ ☆

Name: _____

Prep-Time   Cook-Time   Serves

☐ Breakfast   ☐ Lunch   ☐ Dinner   ☐ Dessert   ☐ O

Ingredients

☐ ....
☐ ....
☐ ....
☐ ....
☐ ....
☐ ....
☐ ....
☐ ....
☐ ....
☐ ....
☐ ....
☐ ....
☐ ....
☐ ....
☐ ....

Directions

1.

2.

3.

4.

5.

6.

7.

8.

9.

10.

Notes

Difficulty: *Easy   Medium   Hard*

Rating: ☆ ☆ ☆ ☆ ☆

Recipe #56

Name: _____

Source:

Prep-Time Cook-Time Serves

☐ Breakfast ☐ Lunch ☐ Dinner ☐ Dessert ☐ Other

Directions

Ingredients

☐ ☐ ☐ ☐ ☐ ☐ ☐ ☐ ☐ ☐ ☐ ☐ ☐ ☐ ☐ ☐

Notes

Difficulty: Easy Medium Hard

Rating: ☆ ☆ ☆ ☆ ☆

Name: _____

Prep-Time	Cook-Time	Serves

☐ Breakfast   ☐ Lunch   ☐ Dinner   ☐ Dessert   ☐ O

Ingredients

☐ ....
☐ ....
☐ ....
☐ ....
☐ ....
☐ ....
☐ ....
☐ ....
☐ ....
☐ ....
☐ ....
☐ ....
☐ ....
☐ ....
☐ ....

Directions

1.

2.

3.

4.

5.

6.

7.

8.

9.

10.

Notes

....
....
....
....
....
....
....
....
....
....

Difficulty: *Easy*   *Medium*   *Hard*

Rating: ☆ ☆ ☆ ☆ ☆

ame: _____

urce:

☐ reakfast   ☐ Lunch   ☐ Dinner   ☐ Dessert   ☐ Other

Prep-Time   Cook-Time   Serves

Directions

Ingredients

☐
☐
☐
☐
☐
☐
☐
☐
☐
☐
☐
☐
☐
☐

Notes

Difficulty: *Easy*   *Medium*   *Hard*

Rating: ☆ ☆ ☆ ☆ ☆

Name: _____

Prep-Time   Cook-Time   Serves

Source:

☐ Breakfast   ☐ Lunch   ☐ Dinner   ☐ Dessert   ☐ O

Ingredients

☐ ....
☐ ....
☐ ....
☐ ....
☐ ....
☐ ....
☐ ....
☐ ....
☐ ....
☐ ....
☐ ....
☐ ....
☐ ....
☐ ....
☐ ....

Directions

1. ....

2. ....

3. ....

4. ....

5. ....

6. ....

7. ....

8. ....

9. ....

Notes

....
....
....
....
....
....
....
....

Difficulty: *Easy   Medium   Hard*

Rating: ☆ ☆ ☆ ☆ ☆

10. ....

ame: _____

urce: _____

☐ Breakfast   ☐ Lunch   ☐ Dinner   ☐ Dessert   ☐ Other

Prep-Time   Cook-Time   Serves

Directions

Ingredients

☐ ....
☐ ....
☐ ....
☐ ....
☐ ....
☐ ....
☐ ....
☐ ....
☐ ....
☐ ....
☐ ....
☐ ....
☐ ....
☐ ....
☐ ....

Notes

Difficulty: *Easy   Medium   Hard*

Rating: ☆ ☆ ☆ ☆ ☆

Name: _____

Prep-Time   Cook-Time   Serves

Source:

☐ Breakfast   ☐ Lunch   ☐ Dinner   ☐ Dessert   ☐ O

Ingredients

☐ ....
☐ ....
☐ ....
☐ ....
☐ ....
☐ ....
☐ ....
☐ ....
☐ ....
☐ ....
☐ ....
☐ ....
☐ ....
☐ ....
☐ ....

Directions

1.

2.

3.

4.

5.

6.

7.

8.

9.

Notes

....
....
....
....
....
....
....
....
....
....

Difficulty: *Easy   Medium   Hard*

Rating: ☆ ☆ ☆ ☆ ☆

10.

ame: _____

urce:

☐ Breakfast ☐ Lunch ☐ Dinner ☐ Dessert ☐ Other

Prep-Time	Cook-Time	Serves

Directions

Ingredients

☐
☐
☐
☐
☐
☐
☐
☐
☐
☐
☐
☐
☐
☐
☐

Notes

Difficulty: *Easy*   *Medium*   *Hard*

Rating: ☆ ☆ ☆ ☆ ☆

Name: _____

Prep-Time	Cook-Time	Serves

☐ Breakfast   ☐ Lunch   ☐ Dinner   ☐ Dessert   ☐ C

Ingredients

☐ ....
☐ ....
☐ ....
☐ ....
☐ ....
☐ ....
☐ ....
☐ ....
☐ ....
☐ ....
☐ ....
☐ ....
☐ ....
☐ ....
☐ ....

Directions

1.
....

2.
....

3.
....

4.
....

5.
....

6.
....

7.
....

8.
....

9.
....

Notes

....
....
....
....
....
....
....
....
....
....

Difficulty: *Easy   Medium   Hard*

Rating: ☆ ☆ ☆ ☆ ☆

10.
....

ame: _____

urce:

Prep-Time   Cook-Time   Serves

reakfast   ☐ Lunch   ☐ Dinner   ☐ Dessert   ☐ Other

Directions

Ingredients

☐
☐
☐
☐
☐
☐
☐
☐
☐
☐
☐
☐
☐
☐
☐

Notes

Difficulty: *Easy   Medium   Hard*

Rating: ☆ ☆ ☆ ☆ ☆

Name: _____

Prep-Time	Cook-Time	Serves

Source:

☐ Breakfast   ☐ Lunch   ☐ Dinner   ☐ Dessert   ☐ O

Ingredients

☐ ....
☐ ....
☐ ....
☐ ....
☐ ....
☐ ....
☐ ....
☐ ....
☐ ....
☐ ....
☐ ....
☐ ....
☐ ....
☐ ....
☐ ....

Directions

1.

2.

3.

4.

5.

6.

7.

8.

9.

10.

Notes

....
....
....
....
....
....
....
....
....
....
....

Difficulty: *Easy*   *Medium*   *Hard*

Rating: ☆ ☆ ☆ ☆ ☆

ame: _____

urce:

□ reakfast   □ Lunch   □ Dinner   □ Dessert   □ Other

Prep-Time   Cook-Time   Serves

Directions

Ingredients

□

□

□

□

□

□

□

□

□

□

□

□

□

□

□

Notes

Difficulty: *Easy*   *Medium*   *Hard*

Rating: ☆ ☆ ☆ ☆ ☆

Name: _____

Prep-Time	Cook-Time	Serves

Source:

☐ Breakfast   ☐ Lunch   ☐ Dinner   ☐ Dessert   ☐ C

Ingredients

☐ ....
☐ ....
☐ ....
☐ ....
☐ ....
☐ ....
☐ ....
☐ ....
☐ ....
☐ ....
☐ ....
☐ ....
☐ ....
☐ ....
☐ ....

Notes

....
....
....
....
....
....
....
....
....
....
....

Difficulty: *Easy   Medium   Hard*

Rating: ☆ ☆ ☆ ☆ ☆

Directions

1.
2.
3.
4.
5.
6.
7.
8.
9.
10.

ame: _____

urce:

☐ reakfast   ☐ Lunch   ☐ Dinner   ☐ Dessert   ☐ Other

Prep-Time   Cook-Time   Serves

Directions

Ingredients

☐
☐
☐
☐
☐
☐
☐
☐
☐
☐
☐
☐
☐
☐
☐

Notes

Difficulty: *Easy*   *Medium*   *Hard*

Rating: ☆ ☆ ☆ ☆ ☆

Name: _____

Prep-Time	Cook-Time	Serves

☐ Breakfast ☐ Lunch ☐ Dinner ☐ Dessert ☐ C

Ingredients

☐ ....
☐ ....
☐ ....
☐ ....
☐ ....
☐ ....
☐ ....
☐ ....
☐ ....
☐ ....
☐ ....
☐ ....
☐ ....
☐ ....
☐ ....

Directions

1. ....

2. ....

3. ....

4. ....

5. ....

6. ....

7. ....

8. ....

9. ....

Notes

....
....
....
....
....
....
....
....
....
....

Difficulty: *Easy   Medium   Hard*

Rating: ☆ ☆ ☆ ☆ ☆

10. ....

ame: _____

urce:

Prep-Time   Cook-Time   Serves

☐ reakfast   ☐ Lunch   ☐ Dinner   ☐ Dessert   ☐ Other

Directions

Ingredients

☐
☐
☐
☐
☐
☐
☐
☐
☐
☐
☐
☐
☐
☐
☐

Notes

Difficulty: *Easy*   *Medium*   *Hard*

Rating: ☆ ☆ ☆ ☆ ☆

Name: _____

Prep-Time   Cook-Time   Serves

Source:

☐ Breakfast   ☐ Lunch   ☐ Dinner   ☐ Dessert   ☐ C

Ingredients

☐ ....
☐ ....
☐ ....
☐ ....
☐ ....
☐ ....
☐ ....
☐ ....
☐ ....
☐ ....
☐ ....
☐ ....
☐ ....
☐ ....
☐ ....

Notes

Directions

1.

2.

3.

4.

5.

6.

7.

8.

9.

10.

Difficulty: *Easy   Medium   Hard*

Rating: ☆ ☆ ☆ ☆ ☆

ame: _____

urce:

Prep-Time　　Cook-Time　　Serves

☐ reakfast　☐ Lunch　☐ Dinner　☐ Dessert　☐ Other

Directions

Ingredients

☐ ....
☐ ....
☐ ....
☐ ....
☐ ....
☐ ....
☐ ....
☐ ....
☐ ....
☐ ....
☐ ....
☐ ....
☐ ....
☐ ....
☐ ....

Notes

Difficulty: *Easy　　Medium　　Hard*

Rating: ☆ ☆ ☆ ☆ ☆

Name: _____

Prep-Time   Cook-Time   Serves

Source:

☐ Breakfast   ☐ Lunch   ☐ Dinner   ☐ Dessert   ☐ O

Ingredients

☐ ....
☐ ....
☐ ....
☐ ....
☐ ....
☐ ....
☐ ....
☐ ....
☐ ....
☐ ....
☐ ....
☐ ....
☐ ....
☐ ....
☐ ....

Notes

....
....
....
....
....
....
....
....
....
....

Difficulty: *Easy   Medium   Hard*

Rating: ☆ ☆ ☆ ☆ ☆

Directions

1. ....

2. ....

3. ....

4. ....

5. ....

6. ....

7. ....

8. ....

9. ....

10. ....

ame: _____

urce:

☐ reakfast   ☐ Lunch   ☐ Dinner   ☐ Dessert   ☐ Other

Prep-Time   Cook-Time   Serves

Directions

Ingredients

☐
☐
☐
☐
☐
☐
☐
☐
☐
☐
☐
☐
☐
☐
☐

Notes

Difficulty: *Easy*   *Medium*   *Hard*

Rating: ☆ ☆ ☆ ☆ ☆

Name: _____

Prep-Time	Cook-Time	Serves

☐ Breakfast   ☐ Lunch   ☐ Dinner   ☐ Dessert   ☐ C

Ingredients

☐ ....
☐ ....
☐ ....
☐ ....
☐ ....
☐ ....
☐ ....
☐ ....
☐ ....
☐ ....
☐ ....
☐ ....
☐ ....
☐ ....
☐ ....

Notes

....
....
....
....
....
....
....
....
....
....
....

Difficulty: *Easy*   *Medium*   *Hard*

Rating: ☆ ☆ ☆ ☆ ☆

Directions

1.

2.

3.

4.

5.

6.

7.

8.

9.

10.

ame: _____

urce:

Prep-Time   Cook-Time   Serves

☐ Breakfast   ☐ Lunch   ☐ Dinner   ☐ Dessert   ☐ Other

Directions

Ingredients

☐ ....
☐ ....
☐ ....
☐ ....
☐ ....
☐ ....
☐ ....
☐ ....
☐ ....
☐ ....
☐ ....
☐ ....
☐ ....
☐ ....
☐ ....

Notes

Difficulty: *Easy*   *Medium*   *Hard*

Rating: ☆ ☆ ☆ ☆ ☆

Name: _____

Prep-Time	Cook-Time	Serves

☐ Breakfast   ☐ Lunch   ☐ Dinner   ☐ Dessert   ☐ O

Ingredients

☐
☐
☐
☐
☐
☐
☐
☐
☐
☐
☐
☐
☐
☐
☐

Notes

Directions

1.

2.

3.

4.

5.

6.

7.

8.

9.

10.

Difficulty: *Easy   Medium   Hard*

Rating: ☆ ☆ ☆ ☆ ☆

ame: _____

urce:

reakfast ☐ Lunch ☐ Dinner ☐ Dessert ☐ Other

Prep-Time   Cook-Time   Serves

Directions

Ingredients

☐
☐
☐
☐
☐
☐
☐
☐
☐
☐
☐
☐
☐
☐
☐

Notes

Difficulty: *Easy   Medium   Hard*

Rating: ☆ ☆ ☆ ☆ ☆

Name: _____

Prep-Time   Cook-Time   Serves

Ingredients

☐ ....
☐ ....
☐ ....
☐ ....
☐ ....
☐ ....
☐ ....
☐ ....
☐ ....
☐ ....
☐ ....
☐ ....
☐ ....
☐ ....
☐ ....

Notes

....
....
....
....
....
....
....
....
....
....

Difficulty: *Easy   Medium   Hard*

Rating: ☆ ☆ ☆ ☆ ☆

Directions

1.
....

2.
....

3.
....

4.
....

5.
....

6.
....

7.
....

8.
....

9.
....

10.
....

ame: _____

urce: _____

Prep-Time   Cook-Time   Serves

☐ Breakfast   ☐ Lunch   ☐ Dinner   ☐ Dessert   ☐ Other

Directions

Ingredients

☐
☐
☐
☐
☐
☐
☐
☐
☐
☐
☐
☐
☐
☐
☐

Notes

Difficulty: *Easy   Medium   Hard*

Rating: ☆ ☆ ☆ ☆ ☆

Name: _____

Prep-Time   Cook-Time   Serves

Source:

☐ Breakfast   ☐ Lunch   ☐ Dinner   ☐ Dessert   ☐ C

Ingredients

☐ ....
☐ ....
☐ ....
☐ ....
☐ ....
☐ ....
☐ ....
☐ ....
☐ ....
☐ ....
☐ ....
☐ ....
☐ ....
☐ ....
☐ ....

Notes

....
....
....
....
....
....
....
....
....

Difficulty: *Easy   Medium   Hard*

Rating: ☆ ☆ ☆ ☆ ☆

Directions

1.
....

2.
....

3.
....

4.
....

5.
....

6.
....

7.
....

8.
....

9.
....

10.
....

ame: _____

urce:

reakfast ☐ Lunch ☐ Dinner ☐ Dessert ☐ Other

Prep-Time   Cook-Time   Serves

Directions

Ingredients

☐
☐
☐
☐
☐
☐
☐
☐
☐
☐
☐
☐
☐
☐
☐

Notes

Difficulty: *Easy   Medium   Hard*

Rating: ☆ ☆ ☆ ☆ ☆

Name: _____

Prep-Time	Cook-Time	Serves

Source:

☐ Breakfast ☐ Lunch ☐ Dinner ☐ Dessert ☐ C

Ingredients

☐ ....
☐ ....
☐ ....
☐ ....
☐ ....
☐ ....
☐ ....
☐ ....
☐ ....
☐ ....
☐ ....
☐ ....
☐ ....
☐ ....
☐ ....

Directions

1.

2.

3.

4.

5.

6.

7.

8.

9.

10.

Notes

Difficulty: *Easy   Medium   Hard*

Rating: ☆ ☆ ☆ ☆ ☆

ame: _____

urce:

Prep-Time   Cook-Time   Serves

□ reakfast   □ Lunch   □ Dinner   □ Dessert   □ Other

Directions

Ingredients

□
□
□
□
□
□
□
□
□
□
□
□
□
□
□

Notes

Difficulty: *Easy*   *Medium*   *Hard*

Rating: ☆ ☆ ☆ ☆ ☆

Name: _____

Prep-Time   Cook-Time   Serves

☐ Breakfast   ☐ Lunch   ☐ Dinner   ☐ Dessert   ☐ O

Ingredients

☐ ....
☐ ....
☐ ....
☐ ....
☐ ....
☐ ....
☐ ....
☐ ....
☐ ....
☐ ....
☐ ....
☐ ....
☐ ....
☐ ....
☐ ....

Notes

....
....
....
....
....
....
....
....

Difficulty: *Easy   Medium   Hard*

Rating: ☆ ☆ ☆ ☆ ☆

Directions

1.
2.
3.
4.
5.
6.
7.
8.
9.
10.

Name: _____

Source:

Prep-Time   Cook-Time   Serves

☐ Breakfast   ☐ Lunch   ☐ Dinner   ☐ Dessert   ☐ Other

Directions

Ingredients

☐
☐
☐
☐
☐
☐
☐
☐
☐
☐
☐
☐
☐
☐
☐

Notes

Difficulty: *Easy   Medium   Hard*

Rating: ☆ ☆ ☆ ☆ ☆

Name: _____

Prep-Time   Cook-Time   Serves

Source:

☐ Breakfast   ☐ Lunch   ☐ Dinner   ☐ Dessert   ☐ C

Ingredients

☐ ....
☐ ....
☐ ....
☐ ....
☐ ....
☐ ....
☐ ....
☐ ....
☐ ....
☐ ....
☐ ....
☐ ....
☐ ....
☐ ....
☐ ....

Notes

....
....
....
....
....
....
....
....
....

Difficulty: *Easy   Medium   Hard*

Rating: ☆ ☆ ☆ ☆ ☆

Directions

1.

2.

3.

4.

5.

6.

7.

8.

9.

10.

ame: _____

urce:

reakfast ☐ Lunch ☐ Dinner ☐ Dessert ☐ Other

Prep-Time Cook-Time Serves

Directions

Ingredients

☐
☐
☐
☐
☐
☐
☐
☐
☐
☐
☐
☐
☐
☐
☐

Notes

Difficulty: *Easy* *Medium* *Hard*

Rating: ☆ ☆ ☆ ☆ ☆

Name: _____

Prep-Time	Cook-Time	Serves

☐ Breakfast   ☐ Lunch   ☐ Dinner   ☐ Dessert   ☐ C

Ingredients

☐ ....
☐ ....
☐ ....
☐ ....
☐ ....
☐ ....
☐ ....
☐ ....
☐ ....
☐ ....
☐ ....
☐ ....
☐ ....
☐ ....
☐ ....

Notes

....
....
....
....
....
....
....
....
....

Difficulty: *Easy   Medium   Hard*

Rating: ☆ ☆ ☆ ☆ ☆

Directions

1. ....

2. ....

3. ....

4. ....

5. ....

6. ....

7. ....

8. ....

9. ....

10. ....

ame: _____

urce:

☐ reakfast ☐ Lunch ☐ Dinner ☐ Dessert ☐ Other

Prep-Time	Cook-Time	Serves

Directions

Ingredients

☐
☐
☐
☐
☐
☐
☐
☐
☐
☐
☐
☐
☐
☐
☐

Notes

Difficulty: *Easy*   *Medium*   *Hard*

Rating: ☆ ☆ ☆ ☆ ☆

Name: _____

Prep-Time	Cook-Time	Serves

Ingredients

☐ ....
☐ ....
☐ ....
☐ ....
☐ ....
☐ ....
☐ ....
☐ ....
☐ ....
☐ ....
☐ ....
☐ ....
☐ ....
☐ ....
☐ ....

Notes

Directions

1.

2.

3.

4.

5.

6.

7.

8.

9.

10.

Difficulty: *Easy   Medium   Hard*

Rating: ☆ ☆ ☆ ☆ ☆

ame: _____

urce:

☐ Breakfast   ☐ Lunch   ☐ Dinner   ☐ Dessert   ☐ Other

Prep-Time   Cook-Time   Serves

Directions

Ingredients

☐
☐
☐
☐
☐
☐
☐
☐
☐
☐
☐
☐
☐
☐
☐

Notes

Difficulty: *Easy*   *Medium*   *Hard*

Rating: ☆ ☆ ☆ ☆ ☆

Name: _____

Prep-Time	Cook-Time	Serves

☐ Breakfast   ☐ Lunch   ☐ Dinner   ☐ Dessert   ☐

Ingredients

☐ ....
☐ ....
☐ ....
☐ ....
☐ ....
☐ ....
☐ ....
☐ ....
☐ ....
☐ ....
☐ ....
☐ ....
☐ ....
☐ ....
☐ ....

Notes

Directions

1.

2.

3.

4.

5.

6.

7.

8.

9.

10.

Difficulty: *Easy   Medium   Hard*

Rating: ☆ ☆ ☆ ☆ ☆

ame: _____

urce:

Prep-Time   Cook-Time   Serves

☐ reakfast   ☐ Lunch   ☐ Dinner   ☐ Dessert   ☐ Other

Directions

Ingredients

☐ ....
☐ ....
☐ ....
☐ ....
☐ ....
☐ ....
☐ ....
☐ ....
☐ ....
☐ ....
☐ ....
☐ ....
☐ ....
☐ ....
☐ ....

Notes

Difficulty: *Easy   Medium   Hard*

Rating: ☆ ☆ ☆ ☆ ☆

Name: _____

Prep-Time	Cook-Time	Serves

Ingredients

☐ ....
☐ ....
☐ ....
☐ ....
☐ ....
☐ ....
☐ ....
☐ ....
☐ ....
☐ ....
☐ ....
☐ ....
☐ ....
☐ ....
☐ ....

Directions

1.

2.

3.

4.

5.

6.

7.

8.

9.

10.

Notes

Difficulty: *Easy*   *Medium*   *Hard*

Rating: ☆ ☆ ☆ ☆ ☆

ame: _____

urce:

☐ Breakfast   ☐ Lunch   ☐ Dinner   ☐ Dessert   ☐ Other

Prep-Time   Cook-Time   Serves

Directions

Ingredients

☐
☐
☐
☐
☐
☐
☐
☐
☐
☐
☐
☐
☐
☐
☐

Notes

Difficulty: *Easy*   *Medium*   *Hard*

Rating: ☆ ☆ ☆ ☆ ☆

Name: _____

Prep-Time	Cook-Time	Serves

Source: _____

☐ Breakfast ☐ Lunch ☐ Dinner ☐ Dessert ☐

Ingredients

☐
☐
☐
☐
☐
☐
☐
☐
☐
☐
☐
☐
☐
☐
☐

Notes

Directions

1.

2.

3.

4.

5.

6.

7.

8.

9.

10.

Difficulty: *Easy*   *Medium*   *Hard*

Rating: ☆ ☆ ☆ ☆ ☆

ame: _____

urce:

☐ reakfast ☐ Lunch ☐ Dinner ☐ Dessert ☐ Other

Prep-Time	Cook-Time	Serves

Directions

Ingredients

☐
☐
☐
☐
☐
☐
☐
☐
☐
☐
☐
☐
☐
☐
☐

Notes

Difficulty: *Easy*   *Medium*   *Hard*

Rating: ☆ ☆ ☆ ☆ ☆

Name: _____

Prep-Time   Cook-Time   Serves

Source:

☐ Breakfast   ☐ Lunch   ☐ Dinner   ☐ Dessert   ☐

Ingredients

☐ ....
☐ ....
☐ ....
☐ ....
☐ ....
☐ ....
☐ ....
☐ ....
☐ ....
☐ ....
☐ ....
☐ ....
☐ ....
☐ ....
☐ ....

Directions

1.
....

2.
....

3.
....

4.
....

5.
....

6.
....

7.
....

8.
....

9.
....

10.
....

Notes

Difficulty: *Easy   Medium   Hard*

Rating: ☆ ☆ ☆ ☆ ☆

ame: _____

urce:

Prep-Time   Cook-Time   Serves

reakfast ☐ Lunch   ☐ Dinner   ☐ Dessert   ☐ Other

Directions

Ingredients

☐
☐
☐
☐
☐
☐
☐
☐
☐
☐
☐
☐
☐
☐
☐

Notes

Difficulty: *Easy   Medium   Hard*

Rating: ☆ ☆ ☆ ☆ ☆

Thank You!

han·gry

/ˈhaNGgrē/ ·adj

The state of anger induced by the lack of food;
An increasingly negative emotional state
triggered by declining blood sugar levels.

CN+J is a small family business. Our continued success depends on delivering meaningful and value-added products. We appreciate all the support our customers bestow upon us such as referrals, buying our products for gifts and reviews on Amazon.

Thank you for your purchase. As a "Thank You" for your continuing support and as a token of our appreciation, below is an QR Code for you to download a free 8x10 PDF printable with the "Hangry" dictionary definition.*

How to scan a QR code from an iPhone or iPad
1. Open the Camera app from on your iPhone or iPad.
2. Make sure the rear facing camera is selected.
3. Position your device to take a photo of the QR code.
4. Center the QR code in the viewfinder (your device should recognize the QR code and display a message).
5. Tap the notification to download your PDF.

Printed in Great Britain
by Amazon